GLASS

Its Many Facets

Kenneth E. Kolb and Doris K. Kolb

ENSLOW PUBLISHERS, INC.

Bloy St. & Ramsey Ave.
Box 777
Hillside, N. J. 07205
U.S.A.

P.O. Box 38
Aldershot
Hants GU12 6BP
U.K.

Library of Congress Cataloging-in-Publication Data

Kolb, Kenneth E.
    Glass: its many facets.

    Bibliography: p.
    Includes index.
    Summary: Describes glass, its physical properties,
how it is manufactured, and its many uses.
    1. Glass—Juvenile literature. [1. Glass] I. Kolb,
Doris K. II. Title.
TP857.3.K58 1988   666'.1   86-32785
ISBN 0-89490-150-8

Printed in the United States of America
10 9 8 7 6 5 4 3 2 1

Illustration Credits:
Bradley University, pp. 10, 33, 36, 38, 41, 47, 49; Corning
Glass Works, pp. 6, 12, 16, 18, 20, 21, 25, 26, 28, 30, 35,
37, 44; Lakeview Museum of Arts and Sciences, p. 13; PPG
Industries, pp. 23, 43; Steuben Glass, pp. 4, 55.

Contents

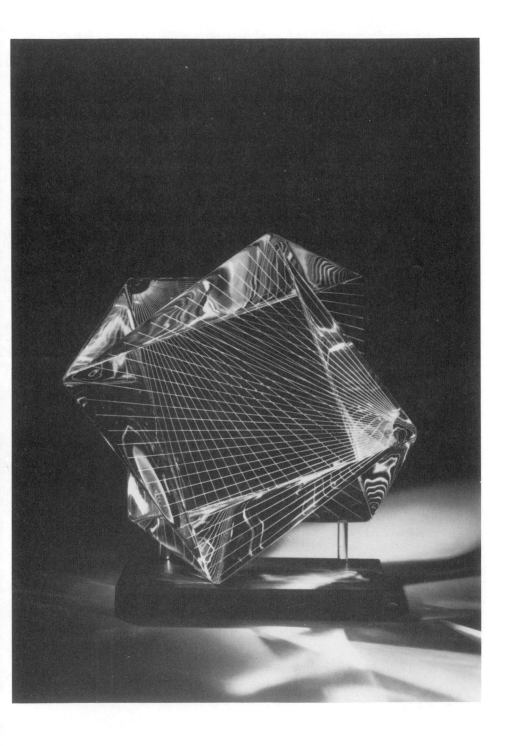

1

The Crystal Palace

The first World's Fair was held in England. The year was 1851, and the place was the Hyde Park section of London. The fair was organized by Queen Victoria's consort, Prince Albert. Although its official name was The Great Exhibition of the Works of Industry of All Nations, it was commonly known as the Crystal Palace Exhibition.

It was held in a gigantic glass building that covered almost twenty acres (81,000 square meters) and looked like an enormous greenhouse. The building required almost a million square feet (93,000 square meters) of window panes, weighing about 400 tons. Since machines for making glass sheet were not to be developed until half a century later, all three hundred thousand glass panes had to be separately blown by hand. At the center of the exhibition was a large, multitiered crystal fountain, an elaborate glass sculpture about twenty-seven feet (8.2 meters) high. There were thousands of exhibits at the fair, but prominent among them were many objects made of glass—goblets, decanters, bowls, pitchers, vases, candlesticks, chandeliers, etc. Some glass was spun into thin threads, which were woven into cloth or fashioned into wigs. A dress of spun glass fabric was made for Queen Victoria.

This famous Crystal Palace Exhibition had a strong stimulating effect on the glass industry, not only in England but all over the world. Within a few years several more crystal palaces were built, one in Dublin (1852), another in New York (1853), and still another in Munich (1854). Before 1850 glass houses had been built as horticultural greenhouses, but now glass shopping arcades and museums started appearing in large cities throughout the world. The demand for glass windows increased steadily, for private homes as well as public

The Crystal Palace in London was a gigantic glass building that had 300,000 hand-blown windowpanes.

buildings. There was also a growing demand for glass bottles, at least partly due to the popularity of bottled soft drinks. More than a million bottles filled with soft drinks were sold during the 1851 Fair.

The Crystal Palace was built by Joseph Paxton, who was a gardener for the Duke of Devonshire. He had become interested in the design of greenhouses, and he had been constructing them for more than twenty years before taking on the Great Exhibition project in 1850. The glass walls for this immense structure were designed so that they would be easy to assemble and dismantle. As a result, the Crystal Palace was erected in only thirty-nine weeks, and after the Fair was over the entire building was taken down and moved to a new location, on Sydenham Hill.

Today glass architecture is common. In addition to thousands of different kinds of greenhouses and conservatories, there are glass office buildings, hotels, cathedrals, shopping malls, restaurants, airport terminals, exhibition halls, recreation centers, and even private houses. The original Crystal Palace no longer exists (it was destroyed during a fire in 1936), but it remains a milestone in the history of glass. It might be said to have ushered in the modern Glass Age.

2

What Is Glass?

You use it every day. When you wake up each morning you probably look at the glass-covered face of an alarm clock, take a peek outside through a glass windowpane, turn on a lamp with a glass light bulb, and then stare into a glass mirror. Perhaps you put on a pair of eyeglasses or a wrist watch with a glass crystal. You may even check out the temperature on a glass thermometer. For breakfast you probably drink orange juice or milk from a glass tumbler, and maybe you have fruit or cereal in a glass bowl. There might be a glass pot of coffee on the table, while the morning news appears on the glass screen of a television set. As you leave home you may get into a car, or a bus, with glass headlights and glass windows all around. The day has barely started, and already glass has played a prominent role in your life.

But what *is* glass anyhow? What is it made of? Actually, glass is a *physical state* rather than a particular composition. Glass is a state of matter with the outside appearance of a solid but the inside structure of a liquid. True solids have a crystalline structure with an ordered arrangement of atoms, rather like the oranges in a neatly packed crate. Glass, on the other hand, is amorphous. There is a random arrangement of atoms, like that of building blocks tossed carelessly into a toy box.

Glass is sometimes referred to as a "supercooled liquid." Consider a liquid such as molasses. When it is hot, it pours easily, but at room temperature it is quite thick and difficult to pour. If you cool the molasses still further, it gets even thicker and harder to pour, until finally it gets so cool it will not pour at all. It has not frozen into crystals; it has simply hardened into a glass. Ordinarily there does not appear to be any liquid "flow" in a sheet of glass. However, it has been found that the windows in very old European cathedrals, after standing in place for hundreds of years, have become slightly thinner at the top and thicker at the bottom.

Did you know that hard candies such as lollipops are glass? They are mainly sugar that has been melted, then cooled to produce a glassy product. Polystyrene plastic is another organic glassy material. The familiar throwaway cups made of clear plastic are, like window glass, transparent and brittle. Step on one of these polystyrene cups, and it will shat-

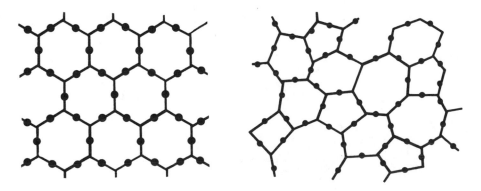

Structure of a true solid and glass compared.

ter just like glass. Transparency and brittleness are two common properties of the glass state.

Polystyrene cups and lollipops may fit the definition of glass, but they are certainly not what glass means to most people. The common material that we call glass is an inorganic silicate, a product made from sand.

Ordinary Glass

When sand is mixed with certain other minerals, melted at a very high temperature, and then allowed to cool, the product is the shiny, brittle material known as glass. The main

The cubes on the left are crystalline sugar; the candies on the right are sugar in its glassy state.

ingredient is sand (silica), but sand is extremely hard to melt, and melted sand is very thick and difficult to handle. The melting point of pure sand is over 1700° Celsius, which is more than 3000° Fahrenheit. If soda (washing soda, sodium carbonate) is added to the sand, the melting point is lowered to about 900° C (or about 1650° F), and the melt is much more pourable and easier to work. Soda has such a low melting point that it will melt in the flame of a match. If melted soda is heated to around 900° C (1650° F), sand will dissolve in it the way sugar dissolves in water. The hot soda-sand mixture will harden as it cools to form a glass. However, this "soda glass" has one major problem. It dissolves in water! To make glass that is durable and water-resistant, lime is also added to the mixture. The lime is usually added in the form of crushed limestone or marble chips. (These are common forms of calcium carbonate, which also occurs in nature as seashells, calcite, coral, and chalk.)

Most glass is made from a mixture that is about two-thirds sand and one-third soda and limestone. The mixture is melted in a furnace until it becomes like thick syrup. Then, upon cooling, it hardens into glass. The process is very much like that for making hard candy, only the temperature is much higher.

In commercial glass furnaces it is common practice to add broken glass, called "cullet," to the mixture of sand, soda, and limestone to be melted. The cullet is usually scrap glass collected from previous melts. Not only does this cut down on waste, but it also improves the melting process, since the presence of the cullet makes the sand easier to melt.

Sand, soda, and limestone were the ingredients used by the ancient Egyptians to make glass, and that same mixture continued to be used all during the Middle Ages. Today hundreds of different kinds of glass are produced, but most glass is still made from that same basic mixture: sand, soda, and limestone. It is known as soda-lime glass, and it is the material used to make most common glass products, such as bottles and windows.

Natural Glass

Man was using nature's glass long before he learned how to make it himself. Arrowheads and knives carved from natural obsidian appear to have been used as long ago as 75,000 B.C. Obsidian is volcanic glass, a kind of granite that was melted during volcanic eruptions and then cooled down so

This picture shows early glassworkers using a glass-melting furnace.

quickly that it did not return to the crystalline state. Obsidian is usually dark gray in color and very brittle. It fractures easily to produce fragments with sharp edges, hence its use by ancient man to make cutting tools. An enormous mass of this volcanic glass, called Obsidian Cliff, is located in Yellowstone National Park. It is about 165 feet (50 meters) high, truly a mountain of glass.

A second glassy material found in nature is pumice. Also found in areas around volcanoes, pumice is solidified volcanic froth. It is low in density because it is full of bubbles. It is really a solid foam in which the "solid" portion is in the glassy state. Pumice is normally used in the form of a fine powder as a polishing material.

A third type of natural glass is produced by lightning. Fulgurites are thin glassy tubes that are formed when sand is struck by lightning, causing the sand to melt. ("Fulguration" is another word for lightning.) They are found along beaches and sand dunes. Often several feet long, they are sometimes referred to as "petrified lightning."

Many ancient arrowheads were made from obsidian, a natural glass.

There is still another type of natural glass that is more difficult to explain. Tektites are small black beads found in many places throughout the world, but especially in the Pacific Ocean area from Japan to Australia. They have an unusual chemical composition that suggests that they are extraterrestrial in origin. Some people believe that tektites came from the moon, and indeed there does seem to be some similarity between the tektites and certain lunar rock samples brought back from the surface of the moon.

Early Man-Made Glass

When, where, or how it was that man first learned to make glass no one knows. It may have happened as long ago as 5000 B.C., possibly somewhere in western Asia. Perhaps it happened purely by chance during the smelting of copper or in connection with the glazing of pottery. All we know is that when the first glass was made there must have been a very hot fire, and some sand must have gotten mixed with seashells, or limestone, and probably some wood ashes.

The oldest dated glass we have is from Egypt and was made around 2600 B.C. Apparently glass was a precious material in ancient Egypt, available only to the very wealthy. The tombs of the pharaohs contained vases, bowls, and jewelry made of glass.

In order to make such glass articles man needed to know not only how to melt glass, but also how to handle and shape it. Molten glass is an extremely hot, sticky, and corrosive material. It is very difficult to handle and to form. Some articles were made simply by dipping clay molds into hot liquid glass, letting the glass cool and harden, and then scooping out the soft clay cores. Bowls, vases, and cups were made this way. Thick, solid objects could be made by casting, simply pouring the molten glass into molds. Using two molds and pressing the molten glass between them, it was possible to make saucer-shaped articles. One technique that seems to have been unique with the Egyptians was the method of fusing. Thin glass rods were softened by heating, then wrapped around molds, so that the hot glass rods fused together to form bowls and vases.

All of the methods just mentioned—dipping, casting, pressing, and fusing—produced fairly thick glass articles. It was not until about the first century B.C. that the revolutionary technique of blowing was discovered. Glassmakers commonly used long rods for dipping into molten glass in order to draw out samples for shaping. It is likely that hollow pipes started replacing the solid rods because of their lighter weight. We can imagine someone blowing into one of those pipes, quite by chance, and producing a glass bubble, just as a child might blow a soap bubble. That probably occurred around 50 B.C. in the area of Syria or Palestine, but the blowing technique soon spread throughout the Roman empire. Glass bubbles could be blown freely, or blown into shaped molds, to create thin-walled, extremely delicate glass objects. The development of glassblowing by the Romans greatly expanded the variety of products that could be made from glass. It also marked the beginning of mass production of glass.

Although we know that the Chinese had glass beads, often in the shape of eyes, as early as the Chou dynasty (1122–256 B.C.), it appears that glass manufacture in China resulted from trade with western Asia and Egypt rather than an independent discovery of glassmaking by the Chinese.

We cannot help but wonder how people who lived thousands of years B.C. ever managed to make objects out of glass. Learning how to handle molten glass at furnace temperatures must surely have been an extreme challenge for those earliest glassworking pioneers.

A fascinating mystery was discovered in the late 1950s in Israel. During a dig at Beth She'arim, an ancient (200 A.D.) village in Palestine, archeologists excavated a cistern and were cleaning off the cover to make a display for a model of the village. The cover was a heavy rectangular slab about 10 feet (3 meters) long, 6 feet (2 meters) wide, and 1½ feet (0.5 meters) thick. It weighed about 9 tons, and it turned out to be solid glass. Analysis has shown it to be a soda-lime glass that would have required a melting temperature of approximately 1000° C (1800° F). Such enormous pieces of glass are very difficult to make. The 200-inch (5-meter) glass disk made in 1934 for the Mount Palomar telescope had to be cooled so slowly (in order to avoid cracking) that it took almost a year to cool. It is considered to be one of the technological wonders of the world. How did they ever manage to make that gigantic slab of glass at Beth She'arim? No one knows. Nor can anyone figure out why they wanted to make it in the first place.

It took almost a year to cool the 200-inch (5-meter) glass disk for the Mount Palomar telescope in order to keep the glass from cracking.

3

Glass Forming Techniques

Glass products are made by forming hot softened glass into desired shapes and then letting them cool and harden. Molten glass has the consistency and stickiness of very thick molasses, but it is as hot as a furnace and very hard to handle. Over the years the skilled workers who knew how to handle glass came to be known as "gaffers." Gaffer literally means grandfather, someone with experience. It takes years of experience to become a really skillful glassworker, or gaffer. Although there are still some glass articles being made by hand today, most glass products are now made by machine. The classical methods of glass forming—casting, pressing, fusing, and blowing— are still used, but often in sophisticated new forms. By way of example, let us look at how glass is formed into three common products: bottles, windows, and light bulbs.

Bottles

The key to making glass bottles was the discovery of the blowing process around 50 B.C. A gob of hot glass was picked up on the end of a long blowpipe, blown into a bubble, and then further shaped and allowed to cool. The gaffers found that whirling their blowpipes during the blowing process would cause the bubbles to elongate into various oval shapes. Pressing flat tools against the bubbles would flatten them, and pointed tools could create indentations and patterns. More controlled shapes were possible if the glass bubbles were blown into clay molds. During the Middle Ages hand-blown glass bottles were used to store oil, wine, medicines, cosmetics, and perfumes.

It was not until the nineteenth century that machines for making bottles began to appear. The machines could carry out certain steps in the bottle-making process, but men still had to feed the glass into the machines and transfer the glass from one step to the next. Glassmakers often used a "press and blow" process that involved first pressing a gob of glass

The mold has just been removed from the large bottle that this gaffer is blowing.

into a jar shape and then blowing it into a bottle-shaped mold.

The first automatic bottle maker, the Owens machine, went into production in 1903. It used a suction device to feed the right amount of glass into the mold. It also used a gas-fired furnace, which allowed much better temperature control than was possible with wood or coal. (In automatic glass-forming machines it is critical that the glass be at the right temperature.) The Owens machine had a number of sets of suction and blow molds laid out in a circle around the center of the machine, from which electric power, vacuum, and compressed air were supplied. The Owens machine worked much like a large hand spray gun: suctioning, then blowing.

Modern machines for making bottles begin by dropping measured gobs of molten glass into molds, where the glass is first formed into rough shapes called blanks, or parisons. Nozzles then blow in compressed air to fill the bottle-shaped molds. When the glass cools and hardens, the molds open up and retract. The finished bottles then pass into a lehr, or annealing oven. Here the bottles are reheated, not enough to melt the glass but enough to allow the glass structure to "relax" slowly. If the glass is not annealed, it may crack from strains developed during the forming process. Some bottle machines can turn out 12-ounce bottles at the rate of 200 per minute.

Windows

Flat sheets of glass are able to keep out noise, dirt, insects, and bad weather, while still letting in light and the outside view. The first glass windows were probably made by the Romans, but their flat glass had very little resemblance to modern window glass. These earliest windows were made by simply pouring melted glass onto stones, or pressing it into shallow molds and letting it harden. The glass was greenish blue in color, and it varied widely in thickness. Then in the fourth century A.D. the Romans started making disks of glass, about 6 to 8 inches (15 to 20 Centimeters) in diameter. These were probably forerunners of "crown glass," a common type of flat glass made during the Middle Ages and up until the nineteenth century.

To make crown glass the gaffer would pick up a large gob of molten glass on the end of a blowpipe and would blow a large bubble. To the hot glass sphere a rod would be attached directly opposite the blowpipe. Then the glass would be allowed to cool, and the blowpipe would be broken off, leaving a hole in the glass globe roughly tulip shaped. The glass would then be reheated, and the gaffer would rotate it very rapidly, causing the hot softened glass to spin. Suddenly, under the force of this rapid rotation, the open end of the globe would flare out, much like the opening of an umbrella, to produce a large disk of glass. After the disk was annealed and cooled, it was trimmed to make a square window pane, or the entire disk could be used as a round window. The glass had a smooth and brilliant surface, but there remained a spot in the center where the iron rod had been attached. Because the

Early glassblowers made disks of "crown glass" by rapidly spinning a globe of molten glass.

20

spot resembled a crown, the glass became known as crown glass. It was also referred to as "bull's-eye" glass. Rectangular windows were sometimes cut from the area of the disk outside of the bull's eye, but they tended to be small, since the entire disk would not be more than several feet in diameter.

To make larger rectangular windows, the cylinder process was the method used for many years. The panes were not so smooth as crown glass, but they were free of bull's-eyes, and the sheets could be made much larger. The hundreds of thousands of sheets of glass needed to build the Crystal Palace were made by the cylinder process. A large hand-blown bubble of glass would be swung back and forth in a deep trench, where it would elongate into a big sausage-shaped cylinder about 5 feet (1.5 meters) long and 15 inches (37.5 centimeters) in diameter. The cylinder was allowed to cool and then split down the side with a hot iron (or diamond cutter).

For many years sheet glass was made by the cylinder process.

The cylinder then went into a flattening oven, where it was softened and flattened out on the smooth stone floor of the oven. The finished sheets were never completely flat or free from waviness, so images seen through them were usually distorted.

The first successful machine for making window glass was the Lubbers machine, built in 1903. Based on the cylinder process, it used a circular iron frame (called a bait) which was lowered onto the surface of a pot of melted glass and then slowly raised, drawing up with it a cylinder of hot glass that hardened as it cooled. The cylinder was then split and flattened. Glass panels measuring 2 feet (0.6 meters) by 6 feet (1.8 meters) could be made with this machine, but it was soon displaced by several different flat drawing machines that used straight iron rods instead of circular baits. The first one began operating in 1913. A long iron rod would be lowered onto the surface of a tank of melted glass and then slowly pulled upward. Since the bait was long and straight, it would draw up a large continuous sheet of hot glass, which was then cooled and cut into panes. During the first half of this century, the drawing process became the standard method for making flat sheets of glass. As recently as 1960 most commercial window glass was still being made this way.

Some flat glass was made by the rolling process. Melted glass was poured onto a long moving table and sent through a roller like pastry dough. The glass sheet made by rolling was never completely smooth, so it usually had to be finished by grinding and polishing. Although no longer used to make plate glass, the rolling process is still useful for making figured glass panels. When designs are cut into the roller surfaces, the rolled glass sheet comes out patterned.

In 1959 the Pilkington Company in England introduced the revolutionary new float process for making high quality plate glass. It is based on the fact that the smoothest thing on earth is the surface of a quiet liquid. Hot glass is allowed to flow onto a pool of hot molten tin. The liquid tin makes the glass smooth on the under side, and the liquid glass is naturally smooth on top. As the glass flows along the surface of the melted tin, it gradually cools down and becomes rigid (although the tin remains liquid in this cooler temperature zone). The rigid glass sheet then leaves the metal pool and passes into the annealing oven. Finally, the annealed sheet is cut into panels and packaged. This is a continuous process that can make superior quality plate glass at the rate of about

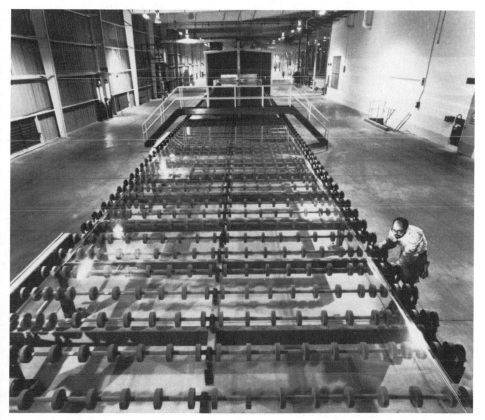

A commercial line producing "float glass."

fifty feet (15 meters) per minute. Since the glass is of such excellent quality and needs no further finishing by grinding or polishing, the float process is by far the most economical way to produce commercial window glass, and most of it is now made this way.

Light Bulbs

Thomas Edison in 1879 made the first electric light bulb, using a hand-blown glass envelope to enclose the electric filament. To this day glass remains the only material for making lamp bulbs, both incandescent and fluorescent. Not only is glass transparent to light, but it is also able to withstand the high temperatures of the extremely hot filament of an incandescent lamp.

When Edison brought his first electric lamps to market in 1881, he greatly stimulated the development of glassblowing machines. The demand for electric lights was enormous, and the glass lamp bulb industry grew rapidly. The earliest lamp bulbs were blown entirely by hand, each gob of hot glass being blown into a paste mold, with the finished glass bulbs being cracked off by hand. Gradually the process was made semiautomatic, until finally around 1915 several completely automatic bulb-blowing machines were introduced. In effect, these machines simply imitated the traditional hand operations, but they did it all mechanically.

Then in 1926 the fantastic Ribbon Machine was developed at Corning Glass Works. This is the machine that is still being used today to make light bulbs. Departing from conventional techniques, this machine is able to turn out more than a thousand glass lamp bulbs every minute. A small two-inch ribbon of molten glass flows from the bottom of a furnace onto a fast moving horizontal track and is met from above by a series of moving air nozzles and from below by a series of molds. As each nozzle starts to blow a bubble, the mold below it closes, and a puff of air blows the glass into the mold, which quickly opens up as soon as the glass becomes rigid. The glass bulbs are then knocked free from the ribbon and carried through an annealing oven. This machine is so fast that it is astonishing to see it in operation. Ordinary light bulbs are produced at the rate of 1000 per minute. When it is making very small bulbs, which are more closely spaced on the ribbon, the machine can produce as many as 2000 per minute! Because these machines are so incredibly fast, there are only about half a dozen of them in the world. These few ribbon machines are more than able to satisfy the world's demand for light bulbs. In fact, in their spare time they also supply the world with Christmas tree ornaments.

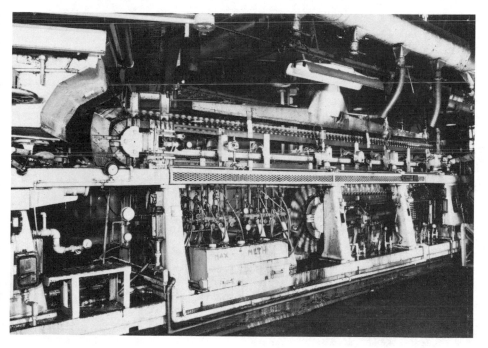

This incredible "Ribbon Machine" can make as many as two thousand light bulbs per minute.

This photograph of the New York City skyline at night shows thousands of glass windows illuminated by glass light bulbs.

Special Kinds of Glass

Although soda-lime glass works well for things like windows and bottles, there are some uses that require special kinds of glass.

Heat-Resistant Glass

Anything made of glass that has to undergo rapid heating or cooling is likely to break if it is made of ordinary glass. In the early days of the twentieth century glass signal lights were used by the railroads. When the hot signal lights were hit by cold rain or sleet, they would often break. A number of serious train wrecks occured because of these damaged signal lights. Today glass signal lights are used not only for trains but also for airplanes, boats, and automobiles. Even though these are hotter, brighter lights than the ones used originally, they do not break in cold or stormy weather because today's signal lights are made of heat resistant glass.

One of the primary heat resistant glasses was developed in 1912 by Eugene Sullivan and William Taylor at the Corning Glass Works. They made a borosilicate glass by replacing the lime ingredient in soda-lime glass with boron oxide. Not only did this glass resist sudden changes in temperature, but it also had excellent resistance to harsh chemicals. At that time the United States was getting its laboratory glassware from Germany, and World War I soon cut off this supply, so some of the new borosilicate glass was fashioned into labware. It was an immediate success, far superior to the German glassware it had replaced. To this day borosilicate glass remains the prime material for making test tubes, flasks, and other laboratory ware. Pyrex (Corning) and Kimax (Owens-Illinois) are common trademarks for heat-resistant glass.

This new glass fascinated Corning's Jesse Littleton, who wondered if it might be used instead of metal for oven cookware. After all, metal reflects heat while glass absorbs it. He cut the bottom from a large glass battery jar and took it home to use as a pie plate. It worked so well that in 1915 Corning

Some glass is so resistant to thermal shock that it can withstand drastic changes in temperature.

28

introduced borosilicate ovenware under the name Pyrex (de-
rived from Littleton's *pie,* so the story goes).

The element aluminum is chemically similar to boron, so
it is not surprising that aluminum oxide also can be used to
make heat resistant glass. Aluminosilicate glass is harder to
melt than borosilicate, requiring a very high furnace temperature (about 1650° C or about 3000° F), but the resulting
glass is quite resistant to heat and chemicals, even more so
than borosilicate glass. Two of the main uses for aluminosilicate glass are top-of-the-stove glass cookware and fiberglass
(about which more later).

The ultimate in heat-resistant glass is silica glass, made by
melting pure silica. The purest form of natural silica is crystalline quartz. It is very hard to melt quartz crystals (they
must be heated to about 1700° C (3100° F) under vacuum),
and the melted quartz is extremely viscous and difficult to
handle and shape. But vessels made from this fused quartz
can be taken from a freezer and placed immediately in a hot
furnace without cracking, much less shattering. Laboratory
glassware made from fused quartz is very expensive, however,
and it is limited to articles that are simple in shape.

A product that is comparable to fused quartz but easier to
make is 96 percent silica. To make an object of 96 percent
silica, the article is first made (a bit larger than desired) from
a special borosilicate glass. The shaped article is given a long
heat treatment and then soaked in hot acid to dissolve away
the soluble borate in the glass, leaving behind a porous glass
that is almost pure silica. The article, which now contains millions of tiny holes, is finally reheated at a temperature high
enough (about 1200° C or 2200° F) to cause the glass to
shrink, completely closing up all the tiny pores. Although it is
only 96 percent silica, this glass is almost as heat resistant as
fused quartz. It is also less expensive, and it can be formed

into much more complicated shapes. Uses for this special kind of glass include projector bulbs and very high temperature laboratory glassware. It is also used to make spacecraft windows, which are subjected to intense and rapid heating when the craft is blasted off through the earth's atmosphere, and again when it plunges back to earth. This 96 percent silica glass is sold under the tradename Vycor.

Lead Glass

The clear, sparkling glass that is used for fine table crystal contains lead oxide in place of lime. Good quality lead glass was first made in 1674 by George Ravenscroft in England. It is highly regarded for its great brilliance and its bell-like resonance. It is more expensive than ordinary glass, but it is easier to make because of its much lower melting point. Lead glasses are heavier than other glasses (the more lead, the greater the density), but they are also softer, which means that they are easier to shape, and simpler to polish and engrave. Their beautiful clarity and high light refraction make lead glasses ideal for making prisms and certain kinds of lenses, as well as for table crystal and art glass. In addition, lead glass has excellent electrical resistance and is used in making various elec-

Lead glass dinnerware adds sparkle and elegance to the dining table.

trical devices, such as the cylinder behind the TV picture tube (in which the television electronics are mounted).

Lead glass normally contains about 25 to 30 percent lead oxide, but there are some very high lead glasses that contain as much as 80 to 90 percent of lead oxide. Radioactive research areas often have thick windows made of this very high lead glass, since lead is an effective radiation shield. When glass contains so much lead oxide, it is extremely heavy and it has a yellowish color. Very high lead glasses are also used as "solder sealing" glasses. These are low melting glasses (some melting as low as 400° C or 750° F) that are used to seal other glasses together.

Colored Glasses

Ancient glass was almost always colored because of natural impurities. Small amounts of certain metal compounds when present in a glass melt can cause the glass to be colored. For example, cobalt compounds give glass a deep blue color, chromium compounds make it green, and manganese compounds make it violet. But making colored glass is more complicated than simply adding the right compound to produce a desired color. There are many things that can affect the color of a batch of glass. Its color may depend upon the composition of the base glass. Nickel oxide, for example, makes soda-lime glass yellow, but it makes potash-lime glass purple. Color can also vary with the ionic charge of the metal being added to a glass. Iron II oxide gives glass a bluish-green color, while iron III oxide makes it brownish-yellow. (The Roman numerals refer to the charge on the iron atoms.)

Even the heat treatment given to a glass may affect its color. When glass is colored with copper oxide, it normally exhibits a blue-green color, but under certain conditions, and with the right heat treatment, a deep red glass is produced. The length of the melting process, as well as any reheating the

31

glass might receive, can help to determine its color. Gases that get into the furnace can sometimes affect the glass color, and radiation treatment can drastically alter the color of certain kinds of glass.

Commercial ruby glass is often made by adding selenium compounds to the glass mix. Selenium gives a red color to ordinary glass but a dark, smoky color to lead glass. A beautiful but rather expensive ruby glass is made by adding a gold compound to a special lead glass. The common brown "amber" glass, widely used for making bottles, contains the element carbon along with iron sulfide. Black glass is usually made by adding manganese dioxide to the glass melt, often along with oxides of nickel and chromium.

Sometimes the problem is not how to put color into a glass but how to take it out. Melted glass almost always contains impurities which tend to give it color, usually greenish. Have you ever noticed that sheets of clear plate glass, when viewed from the edge, are often green? Or have you observed that most old bottles, such as those found in museums, are various shades of green? It is mainly iron impurities that produce the bottle green color that usually results when glass is melted. One way to make glass that is colorless is to start with carefully selected raw materials that are very low in iron and other impurities. A much cheaper way is to add small amounts of color ingredients to ordinary glass to mask the color that is already there. For example, the purple color of manganese can be used to offset the natural greenish yellow in a glass melt. Often a selenium-cobalt mixture is used, the selenium pink and the cobalt blue acting to neutralize the yellow-green color due to iron.

Frosted Glass

One of the unusual chemical properties of glass is its reaction with hydrofluoric acid (HF). The acid dissolves the glass by converting its base material, silica, into silicon fluoride (which is a gas!) and water.

Not only does this reaction produce a gas, but it also gives off a large amount of heat, making the reaction potentially explosive. There has been an occasional tragic accident in which HF has been put into closed glass containers and men have lost their lives in the resulting explosion. Needless to say, you should never try to store HF in a glass bottle! *Plastic* bottles and laboratory ware are normally used for handling hydrofluoric acid.

Glassmakers take advantage of the HF reaction in making frosted glass. When treated with HF, and then rinsed clean, glass is left with a roughened surface that has a foggy or frosted appearance. Most lamp bulbs are frosted (on the inside) in order to reduce glare and improve light diffusion. Sometimes windows and glass building panels are frosted so that they will be translucent (allowing light to pass through) without being transparent ("see through"). Art glass objects are sometimes frosted in order to produce a soft, satiny look.

Ordinary light bulbs are frosted by rinsing the insides of the bulbs with hydrofluoric acid.

An alternative way to make frosted glass, without using HF, is to apply fine silica powder to the hot glass surface just before it is cooled.

The HF reaction is also used for etching glass. One way to scratch patterns into glass is to use a tool called a stylus with a sharp diamond point. Since diamond (a form of carbon) is the hardest natural mineral on earth, it can easily cut into the glass surface. Spinning copper wheels are also used for engraving images onto glass. Another procedure depends on the action of HF. The method involves (1) coating the glass surface with a thin layer of hot wax, (2) letting the wax cool and harden, (3) drawing pictures into the wax-coated surface, and then (4) treating the surface with HF. The glass is eaten away by the HF only along those lines where the wax has been removed in the drawing process. After the HF has been rinsed away, the wax coating is removed. Wherever the wax layer had remained intact, the glass surface remains smooth, while the drawing made through the wax ends up as a permanent etching in the glass.

Opal Glass

The white glass that many people call milk glass is known officially as opal. It normally contains about 5 percent of an insoluble material such as calcium fluoride. Opal glasses are transparent when they are melted, but they become milky as they cool because of many tiny particles (called inclusions) that come out of the melt as it cools. Alabaster glass is a type of opal that is more opaque because the dispersed particles are larger. Alabaster glass is made by adding ordinary table salt to the melted glass.

White glass seems to have appeared first in Venice around the fifteenth century. It became especially popular in Europe during the eighteenth century, when porcelain was very much admired, and opal glass was widely used as imitation porcelain.

Strong Glass

Ordinary glass is rather fragile and easily broken, but it is possible to make glass so tough that it can be used as a hammer. *Tempered* glass is glass that has been heated to its softening point and then quickly cooled. This kind of heat treatment sets up forces in the glass that make it much stronger. A scientist would explain that the glass surface is in a state of compression, and that is what makes it so tough. A coffee mug made of heat-tempered glass can be used to hammer nails. Glass doors and the side windows in cars are usually made of tempered glass because they need special toughness. Tempered glass might be compared with tempered steel. A new steel sword is greatly strengthened when it is heated until it is

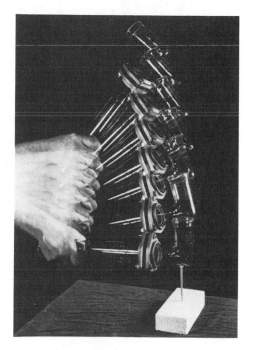

A piece of tempered glass pipe can be used to hammer a nail.

red hot and then suddenly quenched by being plunged into cold oil or water.

The famous Prince Rupert's drops illustrate how strong tempered glass can be. Prince Rupert's drops are made by dropping very small gobs of melted glass into water, where they are cooled very suddenly. The drops, approximately ⅜-inch (1 centimeter) in diameter, are usually pear-shaped with tapering tails. Their outside surfaces are extremely strong because the fast cooling has left them in compression. These odd little beads of glass can withstand being struck with a heavy hammer. However, the glass inside the drops has been left in a weak, unstable condition, so that the slightest scratch can cause the drop to disintegrate. If the thread-like tail of a

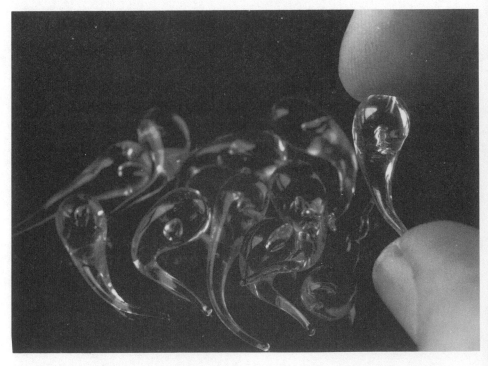

Prince Rupert's drops are strong enough to withstand a blow from a hammer, but if scratched or broken at the tip they disintegrate into powder.

Prince Rupert's drop is pinched off, the entire drop flies apart into tiny fragments.

Glass can also be strengthened chemically. If a strip of a certain glass that is rich in sodium is placed in a bath of potassium nitrate for about eight hours, the smaller sodium ions exchange places with the larger potassium ions. The presence of the larger potassium ions in the glass surface causes crowding (or compression) and the glass becomes stronger. In fact, it is actually possible to *bend* the strip of glass to some degree. Spirals of this glass can be stretched like metal springs. Chemically treated glass sheet has been used in rear windows for folding convertible tops.

Still another way to make glass strong is to use two different kinds of glass, covering one with a coating of the other. By using an inner glass with more expansion and contraction, and coating it on both sides with a glass of very little expansion, a strong glass sandwich is produced. As the hot glass cools, the inner part contracts more, pulling the outside layer with it, so that the surface glass is "crowded," or in compression. This kind of strengthened glass is used to make optical glasses and dinnerware, such as Corelle.

A spiral of tempered glass tubing can be stretched just like a metal spring.

Light-Sensitive Glass

Glass that darkens in strong light but goes back to its original color in the shade is called photochromic glass. It is used in making self-darkening sunglasses and windows for office buildings and hospitals. This unusual glass is based on the fact that certain compounds of silver (silver chloride and silver bromide) are unstable in light and fall apart to produce silver metal. This is the same reaction upon which black and white photography is based, but in the case of photochromic glass the reaction is reversible. In sunlight the silver compounds in the glass break apart, forming atoms of silver metal, which darken the glass. But in the shade the colorless silver compounds are reformed, and so the glass loses its dark color. The process can be repeated over and over.

Optical Glass

The glass that is used to make lenses and prisms (for cameras, microscopes, etc.) is referred to as optical glass. It must be very carefully made since it has to be uniform throughout and as free as possible from bubbles and other defects. There are more than a hundred different recipes for optical glasses, resulting in products with varying powers of light refraction

The photochromic lens on the left has been exposed to UV light, while that on the right has not. It quickly lightens when the UV light is removed.

(bending) and dispersion (splitting). Optical glasses must be highly transparent and chemically and physically stable, but most of all they must be homogeneous. The melted glass must be mixed very thoroughly before it is formed into products, and the finished glass must be ground and polished with great precision.

Safety Glass

Special shatterproof glass, generally known as safety glass, is used in making products such as windshields. Ordinary safety glass is two thin sheets of plate glass glued together by a transparent layer of organic plastic. If the glass is smashed, it tends to hold together instead of shattering because the glass fragments stick to the organic plastic. The plate glass is often toughened by heat or chemical treatment to make the safety glass even safer.

In the extreme case of bulletproof glass, a minimum of four layers of plate glass and three layers of plastic are used, so that a finished window might end up being several inches thick. Such windows find use in banks and jewelry stores as well as airplane windshields and viewers for high pressure chambers.

5

Varied Forms of Glass

Not only can the properties of glass be altered by changing its composition or giving it some type of special treatment, but the physical form of the glass can also be modified.

Foam Glass

When borosilicate glass is ground up with carbon and then heated in a furnace until the glass melts, bubbles of carbon dioxide gas are given off. The carbon reacts with oxides in the glass to produce the carbon dioxide gas, which causes the glass mixture to swell up like a rising loaf of bread. The cooled and hardened product is black (like carbon) and more than 90 percent of its volume is bubbles. Called foam glass, this lightweight material is waterproof, fireproof, and easily cut with a saw. It is an excellent material for insulating the roofs and walls of buildings. Since its foam-like structure makes it much lighter than water, it is also useful for making floats of various types.

Glass Bricks

A glass brick is a hollow block of heat-resistant glass made of two pressed squares held together by a continuous span of glass, so that a pocket of air several inches thick is trapped inside. The dead air space inside the glass block makes it a good insulator against both heat and cold. These glass bricks are used to build outside walls and windows as well as inside partitions between rooms. They are so strong that they can even be used to construct the outside walls of tall buildings.

Glass Beads

While riding in a car at night we sometimes pass bicycles or joggers with strips of reflector tape that seem to be glowing in the dark. Actually the tape does not glow at all. It merely reflects the light from the car headlights. There are millions of tiny glass beads imbedded in the coating on the reflector tape. The beads are too tiny to see, but they are big enough to reflect light.

The stripes down the center and sides of highways are also easy to see at night, and for the same reason. They are painted with glass bead reflectorized paint. As soon as the light from your car headlamps falls on the stripes, it is reflected back to you so that you can see the road for many feet ahead. A gallon of the paint used for traffic stripes contains

Hollow glass bricks are strong building blocks suitable for outside walls.

about 4 pounds of tiny glass beads. Painted stripes containing glass beads are not only much easier to see, but they also last longer because the glass in the paint wears so well.

Highway road signs (the ones that seem to light up as you pass by them) are also painted with glass bead paint. Typically the background paint is green or blue, and the information is spelled out in white. If you look closely, you will see that the letters and numbers in these signs are outlined in large glass beads about the size of marbles. Reflecting glass beads have made night driving much safer than it used to be.

Glass beads are made in many different sizes for a wide variety of uses. They are used to make all kinds of jewelry, used as marbles for games, and melted to make fibers for weaving fabrics. Some glass beads are so small that they act like tiny dust particles. One of the uses for this glass powder is as a thickener for products such as toothpaste.

Coated Glass

A thin coating of metal or metal oxide can give a glass unusual properties. The most familiar metal-coated glasses are mirrors. Mirrors are made by depositing a thin layer of metal on the back of a sheet of glass. Traditionally the metal was silver, but today many mirrors are coated with aluminum. One-way-vision glasses are similar to mirrors, but the film of metal is so thin that it does not completely block out light. To an observer in a dark room looking through the glass into a lighted area, it seems to be transparent; however, to an observer on the lighted side of the glass, it appears to be a mirror.

Iridescent coatings on glass can be achieved by spraying certain metal compounds, such as tin oxide or titanium oxide, onto the hot glass. This technique is often used to make fine art glass that exhibits a rainbowlike display of colors on its surface.

Although glass normally does not conduct electricity, it can be made conducting if it is coated with a layer of tin oxide. Of course, it is only the surface coating and not the glass itself that is electrically conducting. Such glass finds various applications in electronics.

Large volumes of metal-coated glass sheet are used in the building industry to provide office buildings and hotels with glistening mirrorlike walls. Not only are these shining exteriors spectacular in appearance, but they are also practical. They let in sunlight like ordinary windows, but they reflect most of the sun's heat rays.

Glass Fibers

The fine, silky weblike material sometimes called angel hair is really very fine threads of glass. It is one of the forms of fibrous glass generally known as glass wool. It is made by blowing air or high pressure steam into a stream of melted glass. The process is similar to that used for making cotton candy. In order to keep the fibers from rubbing together and breaking, they are usually sprayed with oil as soon as they are made, or sometimes they are coated with resin and pressed into mats. Commercial production of fibrous glass began in

The glass walls of this building are windows on the inside, but they look like mirrors from the outside.

1938 with the formation of Owens-Corning Fiberglas Corporation, which remains the chief producer of glass fibers.

A major use for fibrous glass is insulation. Fibrous glass is used in stoves, refrigerators, water heaters, small appliances, and the walls and roofs of buildings. Since it provides noise insulation as well as heat insulation, it is also used to make acoustical ceiling tile and to insulate automobiles and airplanes. A large passenger plane contains several tons of glass fibers. But there are thousands of other uses for glass fibers, from furnace filters to surgical suture thread.

When fibrous glass is mixed into a suitable resin, and the product is allowed to harden, glass-reinforced plastic is produced. It is a lightweight material with unusual strength and toughness. Although glass fibers are strong, they normally tend to break when they rub back and forth. But the fibers are separated and protected from each other when they are

Thin fibers of glass look and feel very much like silk threads.

surrounded by plastic, and so the various glass-reinforced plastics are remarkably strong. They are used to make furniture, luggage, boats, airplanes, and many kinds of sports equipment. Certain cars, such as the Corvette, are even made from glass-reinforced plastic.

Whereas glass wool is made up of fairly short staple fibers, which are suitable for insulation or plastic reinforcement, these short fibers are not good for weaving into cloth. The long continuous fibers needed to weave fiberglass fabrics are pulled from melted marbles made of aluminosilicate glass. Each glass marble yields a fine continuous thread of glass about 90 miles (150 kilometers) long, enough to stretch from Detroit to Cleveland. Fabrics woven from glass fibers come in a wide variety of colors and weaves, and some of them are amazingly soft and beautiful. Since they are sun-resistant, glass fiber fabrics are especially useful for making curtains and draperies. Because they are fireproof, they are also important for making clothing and equipment for fire fighters. There are many other applications for woven glass fabrics, too, ranging from fine screens used to filter blood plasma to thick tapes used in making orthopedic casts.

Some Recent Developments

Today there are hundreds of different kinds of glass on the market, used to make an almost endless variety of products. Most of the glasses now being made were not available in 1950, and the uses for glass have multiplied since that time. Although many new applications for glass might be considered trivial, glass research has led to the development of some highly important new products.

Fiber Optics

One of the most fascinating uses for glass fibers is in the area of communication. For the past century, ever since the invention of the telephone, copper wire has been used for telephone lines. Sound waves are converted to electrical impulses, which are transmitted through the wire and then translated back into sound at the receiving end of the line. Copper wire works well for this purpose, but now it is being replaced to some extent by glass fibers. A thousand-mile glass fiber telephone line now connects Boston with Washington, D.C., and downtown areas of cities such as Chicago are being rewired with glass fibers. These special glass fibers are called fiber optics or optical wave guides, and they have some advantages over copper wire. The signals carried by glass fibers are not affected by electrical or magnetic fields (which can cause telephone static and scramble computer messages), and glass is not subject to corrosion by environmental pollutants as copper is. But perhaps the most important advantage of glass fibers is their smaller effective size. A ¼-inch (about .6-centimeter) bundle of glass fibers can handle as many messages as a 4-inch (10-centimeter) bundle of copper wires. A cable of glass fibers only half the size of a copper cable can carry many times as much information. This means that rewiring a building or a city with glass fibers can be done without tearing out walls or digging up streets (which would be necessary in order to lay down larger copper cables). The smaller glass "wires" can be snaked through the old copper lines, and they can provide much greater communication while taking up less space.

Does this mean that copper telephone wires will be phased out altogether? Probably not. In small towns and rural areas telephone messages will continue to be carried by copper wires. Telephone transmission through glass fibers is more

The thin glass fibers used as optical wave guides are extremely high in purity and as fine as human hair.

complicated than copper wire transmission. In order to be carried through glass fibers, messages must be in the form of light. An optical wave guide is actually a "light pipe." The sound directed into a telephone must first be converted to an electrical signal, which is then used to pulse a laser so that it gives off light signals. Intermittent bursts of light are the "messages" that are carried by glass fibers. At the end of the line, the light pulses must be transformed back to electrical signals, which are then translated back into sound waves.

In order to transmit light effectively over long distances, glass fibers must be extremely pure and transparent. If the ocean were as transparent as the glass in optical wave guides, we could look down from a boat and see the bottom of the ocean at its deepest point. Making such ultrapure glass requires a special technique whereby highly purified liquids, such as silicon chloride, are vaporized and reacted with steam to deposit very high purity glass. The glass is then drawn out into very fine thread of carefully controlled diameter, and finally it is coated with a tough plastic film so that it will resist scratching and breaking.

Fiber optics are not only being used to replace old telephone lines. Companies are installing glass fiber lines to speed up their own information transfer through computer interfacing. Many other important uses are also being found for fiber optics. In medicine, for example, flexible glass fibers allow internal inspection of many parts of the body without the need for surgery.

Glass Ceramics
If you took a test tube and heated it in a very hot oven (600° C or 1100° F) for several months, the glass would slowly crystallize. It would turn white and become very fragile and crumbly. You might suppose that glass should be stronger in

the crystalline state, but for centuries whenever anyone tried to crystallize glass, the product was weak and useless.

Then in 1957 Donald Stookey at Corning left a piece of glass in a furnace and it accidentally overheated by several hundred degrees. The glass happened to be a light-sensitive sample that contained silver. During the heating process the many tiny particles of silver acted as crystal "seeds" and caused a controlled kind of crystallization to take place. As a result the glass turned into a very strong opaque material. The product was a completely new kind of composition, a glass that had millions of microcrystalline areas spread throughout. It was a super-strong glass ceramic. Glass is noncrystalline, but glass ceramics contain many tiny regions with an ordered crystalline structure. They range from 50 to 90 percent in crystallinity. Normally they contain titanium dioxide rather than silver as the crystal seed ingredient. Glass ceramics are used to make missile nose cones as well as dinnerware, cookware, and range counters. They are also used in automobile catalytic converters.

The clear glass dish on the left contains "seeds" which on heating turn into millions of crystalline areas, producing the strong white dish on the right. (The design is added later.)

Glass ceramics range in appearance from completely opaque to transparent. There is a line of transparent glass ceramic cookware on the market that has a brownish color but is otherwise clear. In this case the microcrystals are so tiny that they do not block out the light, so the product remains transparent instead of turning opaque. Glass ceramics have also been made that are castable (can be poured into molds) and machinable (can be shaped by metalworking tools). They have turned out to be ideal materials for making dental crowns and artificial teeth. Glass ceramics are also being tried out in automobile engine blocks. It even appears that certain kinds of glass ceramic materials may have potential as superconductors.

Surface-Active Glasses

In the medical field glass and glass ceramics are showing promise as biomaterials, to repair broken bones, replace missing teeth, or attach orthopedic prosthetic devices. Special surface treatment allows the glass to attach itself to soft tissue in a living body. These bioactive materials can actually form bonds with the collagen in the host tissue, so that implants become chemically attached to the surrounding tissues. No other implant material has been able to do this. In some cases the surface-active glass has been applied as a coating to implants made of stainless steel, titanium, or other materials, in order to give them bone-bonding capacity.

Another biochemical application of glass involves enzymes. Enzymes are special kinds of protein molecules that catalyze the various chemical reactions occurring in living plants and animals. If a particular enzyme is missing in an organism, the reaction for which it is a catalyst cannot take place. Many genetic diseases involve the lack of a critical enzyme. When enzymes are removed from living cells, they can make the reactions that they catalyze occur in test tubes, or even in large plant reactors, assuming that conditions are favorable. Porous glass can be used as a solid support for these enzymes. The enzyme molecules are attached to the glass with a chemical coupling agent so that they are tied down on the glass surface. In an ordinary batch process in a plant, one batch of enzymes is used to make one batch of product, and then the enzymes are discarded. This makes the process fairly expensive. By keeping the enzymes immobilized on a glass support, they are easily separated from the reaction products, and so they can be used again. Glass-supported enzymes can even be part of a continuous operation. Many different enzymes have been immobilized on porous glass, and they often retain their activity for months. The immobilized enzyme invertase, for example, is used to convert ordinary table sugar to high fructose syrup for soft drink manufacture.

Nuclear Waste Glass

One of the most serious problems connected with nuclear power plants is waste disposal. In the United States alone there are millions of gallons of radioactive waste that have already been produced from existing reactors. Such large amounts of this waste create enormous environmental problems. Since it remains radioactive for generations, it is important that it be disposed of safely. The best way to do that appears to be the glass method. The liquid radioactive waste is not just poured into glass containers, but it is actually converted to glass, or vitrified. The liquid waste is blended with glass-forming ingredients, melted, and then poured into storage containers. The hardened glass hangs on tightly to the waste materials, so that leaching of radioactivity into the ground over the centuries would be minimized. Very deep storage of the glass in rock bed caverns affords still greater environmental protection. Glass is an excellent medium for encasing these radioactive materials because it has long-term durability and resistance to chemical corrosion. Borosilicate glasses are mainly being used for this purpose, but other types of glass, such as lead-iron phosphates, also appear to be suitable because of their superior chemical resistance.

Solar Cells

Solar cells are solid-state devices for converting the sun's energy directly into electricity. Crystalline silicon (the element, not the oxide) has been an important material in the manufacture of solar cells. Since the crystallization of silicon is a painstaking process that requires extremely pure silicon, solar cells made from silicon crystals are quite expensive. However, it has been found that amorphous, or glassy, silicon can also be used to make solar cells. Glassy silicon cells are much cheaper and easier to make. As a result of these inexpensive solar cells, the solar-powered generation of electricity is looking considerably more attractive.

Glassy Metals

Metals in the glass state are among the newest kinds of glassy materials. To convert metals to a glassy state, the hot liquid metal must be cooled very quickly (within a hundred thousandth of a second) in order to avoid crystallization. Glassy metals are usually metal mixtures, and they often include iron. The materials have very high strength and good corrosion resistance, plus outstanding magnetic properties. They have been used to make superior electric motors and transformers.

Glass Lasers

Lasers are instruments that can take ordinary light and produce a beam of coherent light in which all the light rays are traveling in exactly the same way and in precisely the same direction. (The word laser is an acronym for light amplification by stimulated emission of radiation.) One of the most powerful lasers is made of glass containing a little neodymium. Not only is neodymium-glass a highly efficient laser material, but it also has the advantage that it can be cast in large pieces. (Some are as large as a yard (meter) in diameter.) Neodymium-glass is especially suitable for making big, high-powered lasers. It is being used in the huge lasers that have been set up for nuclear fusion research. These giant lasers produce pulses of up to 300 trillion watts.

*****

GLASS! It is older than recorded history, but it is as new as tomorrow. It is hard to imagine what the world would be like without it. And there will undoubtedly be uses for glass in the future that we have not even dreamed about. Glass is a unique material. What we can do with it is limited only by our imagination.

Glass

Glittering crystal of grace and nobility;
Glass jars and bottles of countless utility;
Sturdy glass pipelines of strength and stability;
Slender glass fibers of web-like fragility;
Sheltering windows of clear visibility;
Prisms of excellent light refractility;
Fiberglass fabrics of soft flexibility. . . .
What other product has such versatility?

Glossary

alabaster glass—An opaque white glass.

aluminosilicate glass—A heat resistant glass containing alumina (Al_2O_3) and used to make top-of-the stove cookware or fiberglass.

amorphous—Noncrystalline; without any ordered arrangement of atoms.

annealing—A controlled, partial reheating process to remove any stresses remaining after a glass article has been formed.

borosilicate glass—A heat resistant glass containing boric oxide (B_2O_3) and used to make laboratory ware and oven cookware.

casting—Pouring melted glass into a mold and allowing it to cool and harden.

cobalt glass—Glass with a deep blue color due to the presence of cobalt.

crystalline—Having a highly ordered structure with a repeating pattern of atoms.

Crystal Palace—A gigantic glass building constructed in London in 1851 to house the first World's Fair.

cullet—Broken up scrap glass, which is often remelted and used again. Adding cullet to a new batch of glass makes it easier to melt.

fiberglass—Fine threads of glass that are used for insulation, for making fabrics, or for plastics reinforcement.

fiber optics—Fine strands of glass that transmit light.

float glass—High quality plate glass made by pouring melted glass onto a pool of molten tin.

foam glass—A black, lightweight insulating material made by heating ground glass with carbon.

fulgerites—Thin glassy tubes that are formed when sand is struck by lightning.

fused silica—A highly heat resistant glass obtained by melting very pure sand or quartz.

fusing—Heating rods (or other pieces) of glass until they are soft enough to stick together.

gaffer—A highly skilled glassworker.

glass—A rigid liquid; a material with the outer appearence of a solid but the inner structure of a liquid.

glassblowing—Shaping hot melted glass with air pressure.

glass ceramic—A glass that contains many microcrystalline regions, which tend to make the glass opaque and very strong.

glass wool—A mass of fine glass fibers with the appearance of fleecy wool.

ion—An atom that has lost or gained electrons and has thereby taken on a positive or a negative charge.

lead glass—A beautiful, sparkling glass that contains lead oxide (PbO).

lehr—An annealing oven.

milk glass—Common name for white opal glass.

modifiers—Ingredients added to glass to improve its properties.

obsidian—A glassy form of granite, produced during volcanic eruptions.

opal glass—Milky white glass, or other translucent to opaque glasses.

optical glass—Very homogeneous glass used to make lenses.

optical wave guides—Very pure glass fibers used to transmit laser beam signals for purposes of communication.

photochromic glass—A silver-containing glass that darkens in sunlight and then lightens up in the shade.

potash-lime glass—A glass made from silica (SiO_2), potash

(K_2O), and lime (CaO).

pressing—Pouring melted glass into a mold and then pressing down on it with a second mold.

pumice—Solidified volcanic foam.

ribbon machine—An incredibly fast glassblowing machine, which can make 1000 or more light bulbs per minute from a ribbon of molten glass.

rolled glass—Glass sheet produced by pouring melted glass onto a flat table and rolling it to the desired thickness.

safety glass—A laminated glass made of two thin glass sheets held together by a layer of transparent plastic.

sand—Small particles of rock, larger than powder but smaller than gravel, made up largely of silica (SiO_2).

silica—A network-forming oxide of silicon that is the main ingredient in most glasses.

soda-lime glass—The ordinary kind of glass used to make windows and bottles. It contains silica (SiO_2), soda (Na_2O), and lime (CaO).

tektites—Beads of glass found in nature and believed to have come from outer space, perhaps from the moon.

Further Reading

BOOKS

Barrington, E.H., *Glass Through the Ages,* New York, Penguin Books, 1959.

Bates, Robert L., *Stone, Clay, Glass: How Building Materials are Found and Used,* Hillside, NJ: Enslow Publishers, 1987.

Brooks, John A., *Glass,* New York: Golden Press, 1973.

Burton, John, *Glass: Philosophy and Method,* Philadelphia: Chilton Co., 1967.

Davis, Frank, *Antique Glass and Glass Collecting,* London: Hamlyn Publishing Group, 1973.

Douglas, R.W., and Susan Frank, *A History of Glassmaking,* Oxfordshire, England: G. T. Foulis & Co., 1972.

Encyclopedias: "Glass" articles in *Americana, Britannica, Collier's,* and *World Book.*

Hix, John, *The Glass House,* Cambridge, MA: MIT Press, 1974.

Kampfer, Fritz, and Klaus G. Beyer, *Glass: A World History,* London: Studio Vista, 1966.

Koch, Robert, *Louis C. Tiffany: Rebel in Glass,* 3rd edition, New York: Crown Publishers, 1982.

Lee, Lawrence, George Sedden, and Francis Stephens, *Stained Glass,* New York: Crown Publishers, 1976.

Littleton, Harvey K., *Glassblowing: A Search for Form,* New York: Van Nostrand Reinhold, 1971.

Logan, Harlan, editor, *How Much Do You Know About Glass?,* New York: Dodd, Mead & Co., 1951.

Maloney, F.J. Terence, *Glass in the Modern World,* Garden City, NY: Doubleday, 1968.

McMillan, P.W., *Glass Ceramics*, New York: Academic Press, 1964.

Mehlman, Felice, *Phaidon Guide to Glass*, Englewood Cliffs, NJ: Prentice-Hall, 1983.

Papert, Emma, *The Illustrated Guide to American Glass*, New York: Hawthorn Books, 1972.

Paterson, Alan J., *How It Is Made: Glass*, New York: Facts on File, 1986.

Phillips, Phoebe, *The Encyclopedia of Glass*, New York: Crown Publishers, 1981.

Polak, Ada, *Glass: Its Tradition and Its Makers*, New York: G. P. Putnam's Sons, 1975.

Rogers, Frances, and Alice Beard, *5000 Years of Glass*, New York: Lippincott, 1948.

Savage, George, *Glass*, New York: Octopus Books, 1972.

Tressider, Jane, and Stafford Cliff, *Living Under Glass*, New York: Clarkson N. Potter, 1987.

Zerwick, Chloe, *A Short History of Glass*, New York: Corning Museum of Glass, 1980.

PERIODICALS

"A New Glass House to House the Best of Beautiful Glass" (Corning Museum), *Smithsonian*, Vol. 11 (May 1980), pp. 66-72.

Bates, Robert L., "Glass: A Solid Liquid", *Earth Science*, Vol. 37 (Fall 1984), pp. 22-23.

Chaudhari, Praveen, Bill C. Giessen, and David Turnbull, "Metallic Glasses," *Scientific American*, Vol. 242 (April 1980), pp. 98-100+.

Cheng, Yang-Tse, and William L. Johnson, "Disordered Materials: A Survey of Amorphous Solids," *Science*, Vol. 235 (February 27, 1987), pp. 997-1002.

Companion, Audrey, and Kenneth Schug, "Ceramics and

Glass," *Chemistry,* Vol. 46 (October 1973), pp. 27-31.

Johnson, William B., "The Coming Glut of Phone Lines" (fiber optics), *Fortune,* Vol. 111 (January 7, 1985), pp. 96-100.

Kihlstedt, Folke T., "The Crystal Palace," *Scientific American,* Vol. 251 (October 1984), pp. 132-143.

Klein, R.L., "Our Priceless Heritage of Glass," *American Home,* Vol. 76 (June 1973), pp. 58-59.

Koepp, Stephen, "London Calling on a Beam of Light" (fiber optics), *Time,* Vol. 129 (January 19, 1987), p. 52.

Koplos, Janet, "Art with Glass," *Horizon,* Vol. 28 (January-February 1985), pp. 9-16.

Lucky, Robert W., "Message by Light Wave," *Science 85,* Vol. 6 (November 1985), pp. 112-113.

Phillips, James C., "The Physics of Glass," *Physics Today,* Vol. 35 (February 1982), pp. 27-33.

Rastorfer, D., "New Glass Technology: The Miesian Vision Surpassed," *Architectural Record,* Vol. 174 (December 1986), pp. 22-23.

Robinson, D.A., "Glass—A Material for Today," *Chemistry,* Vol. 47 (July 1974), pp. 10-14.

Sennett, Richard, "The Glass Age" (lecture on architecture), *Harper's Magazine,* Vol. 272 (June 1986), pp. 14-19.

Stavro, Barry, "Therefore, be bold" (fiber optics), *Forbes,* Vol. 136 (September 23, 1985), pp. 115-116.

Teitleman, Robert, "Rock of Ages" (glass for nuclear waste), *Forbes,* Vol. 132 (September 12, 1983), p. 191.

Teitelman, Robert, "The Optical Connection" (fiber optics), *Forbes,* Vol. 136 (September 23, 1985), pp. 183, 186.

Ware, Leslie, "Forever Flowers of Glass and Magic" (Harvard's glass flower collection), *Audubon,* Vol. 89 (May 1987), pp. 96-109.

Weisburd, S., "Largest Melt from Lightning Strike," *Science News,* Vol. 130 (October 11, 1986), p. 231.

Index